I QUIT MY JOB

TO HELP YOU

QUIT YOURS

YOUR PLAN TO *LEAP* FROM
EMPLOYEE TO **ENTREPRENEUR**

BY STEVE BULLER, CPA

ISBN-13: 978-1539894162

CREATESPACE PUBLISHING

WWW.CREATESPACE.COM

COPYRIGHT © 2016 BY STEVE BULLER

Introduction

"Know thyself." – Socrates

If you're the kind of person who wants to leave the corporate environment and finally live your life on your terms... this book will create your roadmap to freedom! I recognize that this is a rather bold claim, but I wouldn't say it if I didn't believe it. I think there are two kinds of people in the world: Employees dedicate their lives to someone else's vision, and entrepreneurs to their own. I am on a crusade to help people break their golden handcuffs and get to their lives' work.

If you feel like you're floating through life with a 9-5, but you want to have a bigger impact, more freedom, and real control over your destiny, then you need to create your own path. If you feel like you aren't sure how you ended up where you are, and you wish you had made some different choices in the past, it's not your fault. Our education system has trained us to be good little employees, soldiers, consumers... zombies.

Now I will make a quick concession: If you enjoy your job, or your job is easy and you enjoy shutting your mind off for eight hours a day, then you should stay where you are. Otherwise, so many people talk about going out on their own, but they don't because they're afraid. They're afraid because they feel safe and secure at their job... Without any sugar coating, here's what I think about the reason that most people stay at their job:

Security – *the state of being free from danger or threat.*

We all need to wake up and realize that we are not the baby boomer generation. Employers aren't giving pensions anymore, and the pace of change in our country, and the world, is increasing. Our government is printing money that is no longer tied to anything of value. We need to create something of real value if we want to feel secure.

So, what is real value? Allow me to "illustrate" this with a quick story from my childhood...

My brother Jason and I collected comic books when we were young. I remember one of my friends telling me how much an issue of Superman #1 was worth then (today it's up to $3 million). This was my first lesson in investing, and I wanted to put my newfound knowledge to work. That summer, I was out shopping for my birthday with my mom, and I saw the comic book Spawn #1. Obviously, I had to have it.

I asked for it for my birthday, and my mom questioned the $30 purchase, which would basically deplete my birthday budget. I was a little annoyed, so I briefly educated my mom on how much it could be worth in a few years. I'll never forget what she said: *"A thing is worth only what someone will pay for it."* I may still have that comic book floating around in my mom's attic or something, but I guarantee it's not in perfect shape, and, if it was, it would be worth around $15.

The lesson from this story is that value is defined by the owner. And I believe this fundamental concept is at the heart of business. How does any business survive? Its customers value its product higher than the company does. This concept of two people coming together in an exchange that leaves them both better off is my obsession.

If you've been working at a job, then you have specific knowledge. And I'm here to tell you that **your knowledge has value**. Years ago, the famous business guru Peter Drucker talked about a "knowledge society," in which the primary mode of value creation would be brains instead of brawn.[1] Today we live in the "information age," so I think it important to distinguish between these two. Here's how I think of them:

> **Information** – The facts of the matter. If I Google "what causes headaches," I get > 20 million results. That's a lot of information.

> **Knowledge** – Interpretation of information in a useful way. If I was a doctor, I would have lots of information on headaches in my head. That, combined with patterns I've seen and critical thinking, I could help my patient with her headache.

Drucker said that "the knowledge society will inevitably become *far more competitive* than any society we have yet known… There will be no 'poor' countries. There will only be ignorant countries. And the same will be true for individual companies, individual industries, and… the individual, too." He also said that "[organizations] need the knowledge worker far more than the knowledge worker needs them."

We are in this knowledge society now, and it is our individual responsibility to develop our own knowledge and to ensure that it is used for the most benefit to ourselves and others. The good news is that working in a specific industry gives you a depth of knowledge that can be extremely valuable. The bad news is that training in this way leaves you lacking the breadth of knowledge you need to unleash your potential.

Then it's decided. We need to fill in any gaps in our knowledge, package it in a useful way, and find those people who can benefit from it the most. This may sound intimidating, but it's not as hard as you may think. In the *"Back Of The Napkin"* chapter, we will look at the simple concept behind a valuable knowledge business.

This book, or anything I create, is not a "get rich quick" scheme, however. It focuses on fundamental concepts that will take time to learn, implement, and master. If you truly want to transform your life, it requires a paradigm shift from using your knowledge to earn money at a defined hourly, or annual, rate to investing your time up-front, earning little or nothing, to create much larger earnings in the future. To get a look at my first experience with **front-loading** like this, let's jump back into my childhood.

When my brother and I were a little older, we had a neighbor who was not in the best of health, and she had neglected her lawn for some time. She needed two strapping young men to get it back into shape; instead, she got us. When we arrived on that first Saturday, her property looked like something out of *Jumanji,* and we sweat for four hours mowing and weed-whacking... heck maybe there was a machete in there somewhere.

I remember thinking she gave us a lot of money, but I also recognized how hard the work was. We got her property in good, but not great shape, so we came back the following weekend to finish the transformation. After that, we only needed to come by every other week. Now, we were still getting paid by the hour, but boy was that hourly work easier. I learned then that keeping something—like a lawn, my body, or skill—was easier than getting it there in the first place.

I also learned that, if I was willing to invest my energy to do something hard up-front, it could have great pay-off later. And the reality is that most people are unwilling to do this. If they don't see the immediate reward to their work (i.e. a paycheck), they can't see the larger potential down the line. This is a huge, and vital, shift in how we must think: We must invest our time and money into something that will have much larger returns in the future.

For those of you thinking that this is what people do when they draw a paycheck and put it into their 401K or some other paper asset, I would challenge you to consider the predictability and magnitude of that return. Investing in real resources like gold, oil, or real estate may be wise in some cases, but often the start-up capital required is immense, and the timeline for return is long. That's why I'm talking to those people who want actual control over their investment. I think your best bet is to create a business around the knowledge in your head.

Are you ready for the really good news? You've already done the hard work, which is developing knowledge about something. If you're not passionate about the knowledge you've acquired at your job, the concept of the knowledge business applies to anything. There are tons of people out there who want to learn to cook, play guitar, jump higher, and almost everything else under the sun. You just have to decide **who can benefit** from what you know, and then keep them in mind with everything you do. As we move forward, let's call the subject of knowledge that you want to bring to the world your **wheelhouse.**

Starting your own business isn't as hard as you may think, but many people are intimidated because we never learned these skills in school. Profiting in your own business isn't as hard as you may think either, but we all hear about the failure rates of small businesses. The main driver of these failures is a lack of up-front planning, so that's where we're starting with this book. You're going to learn how to plan your knowledge business, and you can start it on the side in your spare time, with minimal time and money investment, until it can support you. How's that for security?

I want to be the most authentic person you'll ever meet, and, if this book is the first you've heard of me, I want to start to develop a relationship. That's why this book tells part of the story about how I planned the business that is relevant to this book. A bit circular I know, but stick with me. My business plan has changed, and it will change again, but I hope you find my story useful. I'll share my thought process, desires, and fears, and maybe you'll be able to relate or even gain some insight.

Let's start the story somewhere in the middle... After a decade in "Corporate America," I finally made the leap to focus my full time shaping the world in my own image—this is my favorite definition of an entrepreneur. In hindsight, when my first full-time employer effectively pushed me out, I should have taken a hint... Instead, it took working at three more companies to make a few conclusions:

- I work better when I can easily see the impact I'm having on people
- I was following an obsolete career path that says "get good grades, go to a good college, get a good job, get promotions, invest in the stock market, retire"
- Most importantly, there are a lot of other people who feel the way I do

I slowly realized that a "good job" and "retirement" were not for me. I much prefer the idea of working at something that I'm good at, I get satisfaction from, and I can make a positive impact on others with. If I'm able to achieve this, then work, weekends, vacation, and retirement all kind of blend together into **life**. I can mean it when I say that I'm "living the dream," which seemed a very common, sarcastic remark in the corporate world.

In graduate school, I had an internship at the firm I would start at after graduation. It was during "busy season," and interns got paid hourly. This meant that an intern would make more than a salaried staff worker in his first or second year. I remember thinking it was great that I was making more money than I ever had before, but I soon wondered "what's the point of making money if I can't enjoy it?" Moreover, what's the point of any of this if I can't **live my own life?**

As the years passed, I climbed the corporate ladder steadily, but I realized that the game I had chosen to play would only end in one way: I would feel chained to my desk and not really enjoy the activities that consumed more of my life than any other. So, while I was employed, I was always learning, working on side projects, and trying to find a way to get out on my own.

The real "ah hah" moment happened when I saw how I could **combine my strength with my passion**. My strength was in finances and the inner workings of a business. My passion is the concept of two people coming together such that both are left better off. Again, quoting Peter Drucker, "the purpose of business is to create and keep a customer." My passion, my obsession, is business. I love helping people bring their true brilliance to the world. If we were all in a position to work at our true strengths, wouldn't we be better off? Wouldn't our impact on others be more positive?

According to a survey published by the University of Phoenix Business School, 39% of employees want to start their own business. So why do so few actually do it? "Many potential entrepreneurs have great ideas and a strong understanding of specific industries, but often do not have the business background to turn concepts into profitable ventures," said Michael Bevis, director of Academic Affairs for University of Phoenix and faculty member for the School of Business.[2]

When I looked at my strength, passion, and the need out there, my mission became clear. I am on a crusade to help others break free from the golden handcuffs, dedicate their lives to something they can be passionate about, and impact the world in their own way. I will do whatever it takes to help those who have the desire to make the leap from employee to entrepreneur.

It takes time to "know thyself," but it's worth putting in constant effort as we go through life. I know that if you're reading this book right now, you have some brilliance that you want to share with others. My goal is to help you build a successful business around your wheelhouse by removing those intimidating, devilish details. We'll find your strength, passion, and those who need you, and we'll build a roadmap straight to them. Let's do great things together.

Call To Action

Throughout the book, I'll include **"calls to action"** which are designed to invite you to learn more and to develop our relationship further, so keep an eye out.

My goal is to show you the best path for starting your business. I'm constantly creating better ways to accomplish this and am excited to share them with you.

Table Of Contents

Introduction 3

Table Of Contents 11

About This Book 12

Inspiration 16

Back Of The Napkin 19

The Business Plan 23

Cover Letter 27

Summary 30

Company 33

Product/Service..36

Market...40

Strategy 47

Team 59

Finances 64

Exit Strategy 71

Appendices...74

Conclusion...76

Notes..78

About This Book

"Plans are nothing; planning is everything." – Dwight D. Eisenhower

This book is about how to plan a business based on the knowledge already in your head. Whether this is from your education, work experience, or hobbies, you've already done the work to acquire the knowledge. But notice that I said this book is about how to plan a business, not how to write a business plan. If you work through this book, you'll be able to write an amazing business plan by the end of it, but that is a by-product in my eyes. The important thing is to go through the exercise to set your business up for success.

If, down the line, you want investors or partners for your business, then having that business plan can be very useful. But if you can show them a business that's already profitable, that's even better. Even on a small scale, if you have a working formula, then it's easy to show how you could multiply it. That's why I say the exercise is the important part. You will work through the details to make your business idea a reality. Then, as you receive feedback from customers, investors, your mother, whomever, you can adapt your plan to suit a changing world.

This life is about progress, not perfection, so it's important that we don't just read and learn, but we implement as well. This book is for people who really want to make the leap from employee to entrepreneur, from 9-5 to life. This book will include **exercises** throughout it, and I need you to commit right now to complete them. Don't worry that your answers might not be exactly the same when you launch your business. Just use your current vision and the guidance in this book. This will accomplish the following:

- Help you learn the concepts and cement them in your mind
- Solidify your plan and start to make it real
- Give you a roadmap to make your business come to life

A famous study by the Small Business Administration division of US Bank discusses the top factors for small business failure. The top general business factor, sited in 78% of the study's failures, was the "lack of a well-developed business plan, including insufficient research on the business before starting it."[3]

I'm emphasizing the importance of planning before jumping into your business, but we don't want to be perfectionists either. Once you know your audience and determine your wheelhouse, get your offer in front of them as quickly as possible to test and receive feedback. I would much rather sink a few hours and dollars up front planning to realize that the idea needs some tweaking than discover this much further down the road. But, like Reid Hoffman, founder of LinkedIn said, *"If you are not embarrassed by the first version of your product, you've launched too late."* It takes a thoughtful mind to balance these two perspectives... Are you up for the challenge?

One of my mentors gave me the great advice to start my business while I still had a job. The ultimate goal of this book is to help you plan a business that you can be happy with both the impact it has on others and the lifestyle it provides for you. If you're anything like me, you may feel like you can't wait to be free of your job. I feel your pain and ask that, at least at the start, you embrace the **power of and**: Be an employee AND an entrepreneur. I believe that anyone can find time to put into action the process that this book covers, while maintaining the "security" of a job.

To build a successful business, you need specific, in-demand knowledge. You have the lion's share of this already in your head, but you may need to educate yourself additionally to fill in gaps, create a plan, and build a business. I hope this book makes you want to start drafting up your resignation letter, but, as I mentioned, I don't recommend you quit your job tomorrow. Instead, use this book to develop a real plan to transition. In that time, maintain your income, and start investing in your brain and your business until you're ready to break the chains of the 9-5.

Does this sound like you? Then read on...

Call To Action

If this book is for you, then you may want to meet others like you. There is nothing more powerful in this world than a community working towards a shared vision.

If you want to meet like-minded individuals for support and connection, request access at the link below. Come join for community, support, and maybe even your future business partner!

Visit facebook.com/groups/starttosuccess

Exercise

1. What is your wheelhouse?

2. Whom can you help?

3. Why do you want to help them?

4. Why are you the right person to teach them?

5. What is the #1 thing they want to learn from you?

6. How will you feel if you help just one person accomplish this?

Inspiration

*"Far better it is to dare mighty things, to win glorious triumphs,
even though checkered by failure, than to take rank with
those poor spirits who neither enjoy much nor suffer
much, because they live in the gray twilight
that knows neither victory nor defeat."*

Theodore Roosevelt

Inspiration is paramount. This quote basically sums up how I feel about life in general. If it resonates with you, I want you to come back to it whenever you feel like you need that spark again. If you've decided to be an entrepreneur, there will be difficult days ahead. There will be amazing ones as well, but it will be a rollercoaster. I just remember that, without the lows, I can't truly appreciate the highs, and I'd rather be feeling both than submit to a mediocre life.

Inspiration is vital to your business, because it drives **passion and curiosity**. When you're passionate, you summon courage instead of running away when the going gets tough. When you're curious, you put in the hours of hard work necessary for any successful venture. When you're inspired, you recognize that you have an impact on something larger than yourself, so you eagerly play your role.

Setting a strong foundation for your business begins with **clarity of mind**. You will be surrounded by distractions and other peoples' priorities. Allow yourself to be receptive to feedback and, of course, considerate of others, but remember that you are the one that will struggle and prosper with your business, so you must hold yourself accountable for making the decisions that matter.

For further inspiration, look at the Intuit 2020 Report on twenty trends that will shape the next decade.[4] Though this was published in 2010, some things are proving truer and truer... One of the sections is titled "You No Longer Need Cash to Start a Business." My biggest take away from this section is the shift from fixed-cost to variable-cost business models. You can plan your business to pay a low, monthly fee for cloud storage instead of investing in redundant hard drives, pay credit card transaction fees only when you make money, and avoid up-front capital requirements. It costs virtually nothing to start your knowledge business.

At the risk of beating a dead horse, let's look at one more angle of the "security" that comes with a paycheck. Consider that one piece of advice from billionaire Warren Buffett is to "never depend on single income. Make investment to create a second source." I think that allowing one's entire earnings and livelihood to be at the mercy of one employer is riskier than the alternative, especially as we look to the future. If this doesn't qualify as inspiration, let it be motivation! Start your business on the side, and you'll soon have two sources of income.

Exercise

1. What inspires you? (So much to be inspired by...)

Back Of The Napkin

"Make things as simple as possible, but not simpler." – Albert Einstein

Obviously, the title of this section is more of a metaphor, but if I I had to literally create a business plan for your knowledge business on the back of a napkin, here is what it would look like (although maybe not quite this neat...):

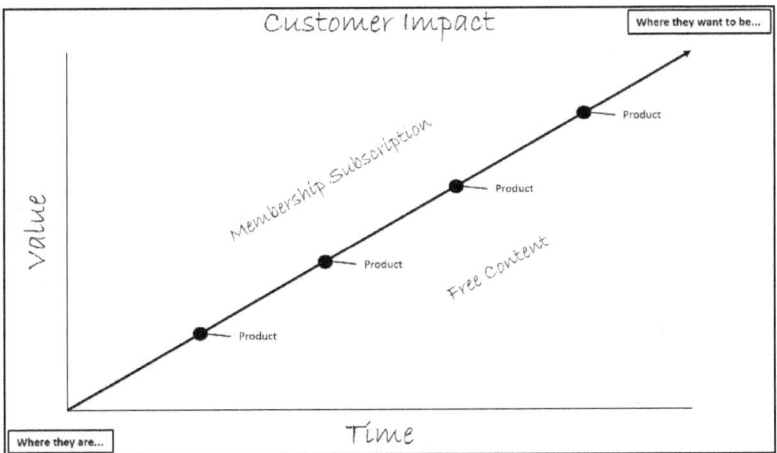

This is the reason that any business succeeds and that anyone buys anything. It's not because it's shiny or fast, because their friend has it or it's the latest release, because they've been buying it for years or it tastes good. These may indeed be underlying reasons, but the overarching reason people buy is because they believe the product will give them a future they desire. Your goal is to take them to their future as it relates to your wheelhouse.

Let's break down the napkin a bit:

- Customer Impact
  Again, this is the whole point of a business. We want to focus on the group of people that we are best suited to teach, inspire, motivate, or help however they need. If we always have them in mind, the rest will follow.

- Value
  It's important to recognize how subjective this word is. Different people value things differently. Focus on your audience, and consider what has high **perceived value** to them. You may be surprised to find that your customers find very high value in some knowledge that you've been taking for granted.

- Time
  We have some goal for our customers to go from where they are to where they want to be in the context of our wheelhouse. We have to remember that what's really important is our customer's goal. For some, the timeline will end after our free offering. For some, it will never end, because they want to remain members in our community. Our goal is to make available the right opportunities for the right customers.

- Products
  Customers are more likely to purchase from a brand that they're comfortable with. If we can demonstrate a lot of value with a free product, then they're more likely to buy a paid one from us. As we move along our timeline, the customer receives more value, we charge higher prices, and both parties are happy. There are as many product formats as you can imagine, but common ones are below (in ascending value order):

- Books, including audio
- Webinars and videos
- Recorded online courses
- Live online courses
- In-person seminars
- One-on-one consulting

- Membership Subscription
  If you're focused on a niche group of people, it makes a lot of sense to create a community around them. One of the most predictable forms of income can be recurring revenue from membership subscriptions. As long as we continue to add value on a regular basis, our customers will gladly remain members. We just need to be creative and listen to what content actually keeps them engaged month after month.

- Free Content
  Whether this is in the form of emails, social media, or giveaways, giving some things away for free will show your customers how much they mean to you, and it's a fantastic way to market and ease new customers into your business.

If we can fill out this napkin, we can build a profitable knowledge business. We design it in such a way that our customer naturally works through our products, ascends in value, and achieves the outcome he desires. I hope this is simple, but not too simple. Just remember that simple does not mean easy. If you want to create something of real value, it will take hard work. I am reminding myself of that just as much as you!

Exercise

You can create a map of your business right now. Use this exercise as the back of the napkin. Don't think about how you will create everything yet; just think about what you want to create.

1. Where are your customers now?

2. Where do they want to be?

3. What kind of products do you want to create?

4. What is your highest value product, that will help your customers the most?

5. What kind of on-going content could you create for your members?

Call To Action

I made a video that covers the back of the napkin concept in more detail. Head to the link below to watch for free and learn more!

Visit iquitmyjobtohelpyouquityours.com/back-of-the-napkin

The Business Plan

Tony Robbins

The remainder of this book will cover all the sections that a traditional business plan document would have. For your knowledge business, you may not need this document yet. Then the rest of this book is worthless? No! Again, the value you will get in understanding the different angles of your business and working through the related exercises is immense.

Once you have this map for your business, you can easily plot your daily activities to get where you want to go. And, down the line, you may want a partner or investor to scale your knowledge business, so it won't hurt to have a head start on your presentation. Complete these exercises as if you were at that point of presentation. And remember that some of this is to expose you to what you need to accomplish; don't expect to have all the answers, yet...

When I was forming my business, I knew what I wanted to do, but I didn't really know how to do it. I had some serious decisions to make, and my thought process looked something like this:

1) I knew I had to play to my strengths, so I needed to leverage my knowledge in finance, accounting, and marketing.
2) I wanted to start something by myself and that took very little capital at first, so I could complete the "feedback loop" cheaply.

3) From reading *Awaken The Giant Within*, by Tony Robins, I knew freedom was one of my highest values, so I needed a way to work from anywhere.
4) I'm most in "flow" when I can work on projects that have a similar nature but vary in detail. I love developing mastery this way.

Considering these pieces, and maybe seven... thousand more that were running through my head, I decided to consult (2) with people starting a variety of businesses (4) to help them plan and set up the infrastructure (1), which I could do anywhere with today's technology (3).

I got my first few clients through word of mouth, while I was still working full-time. But the game changer was when I decided to turn this into a knowledge business: I would master my consulting process and then package it into various digital formats. This would allow me to reach a wider audience, and I could still spend time working one-on-one, as long as I enjoy it.

Now that's the overview, or back-of-the-napkin plan I had. But a lot more thought went into how I would accomplish this: I needed to consider legal ramifications, budgeting and forecasting, marketing myself, and plenty of other details. And that's where a business plan is invaluable.

As you work through the different sections, keep in mind your audience and your wheelhouse. Become one of your future customers, and ask what you really want. If you're always thinking of the people you're trying to help, then you'll know what to deliver.

Here are the sections of your business plan:

- Cover Letter
- Summary
- Company
- Product/Service
- Market
- Strategy
- Team
- Finances
- Exit Strategy

If it sounds like a lot, keep in mind the "back of the napkin" idea throughout it all. These are just different angles to look at your business. You need some broad knowledge about all of them, so you can see your business in the right light. Sometimes, you will need to focus on innovating a new product. Sometimes, hiring for the team will be paramount. Sometimes, your focus should shift to marketing. If you build a foundation of knowledge, even if you don't know everything, you'll at least know what you need to learn next.

Exercise

If planning your business is going to set you up for success, one big prerequisite to this is defining "success" for yourself. Do not confuse your definition with anyone else's. The below questions will help you paint a picture of your successful business. Consider 1, 5, 10 etc. years into the future. This will help you drive towards a real destination, but remember that life is about the journey, so be sure to enjoy the view along the way.

1. What is your mission?

2. What do you want to be known for?

3. What kind of a team do you want?

4. What kind of daily work do you want to focus on?

5. Where do you want to work?

6. How much money do you want to make?

7. What do you want to do outside of your business?

Cover Letter

"We don't know where our first impressions come from or precisely what they mean, so we don't always appreciate their fragility."

Malcom Gladwell

For a long time, my cover letter has been my resume. I realized that my resume said a lot about what I'd been doing over the years, but it said very little about whom I was. I started thinking a lot about what I wanted to be known for. I thought about whom I was best suited to help and how I could reach them. In any situation, I know it's important to put my best foot forward.

Many argue that you have about seven seconds to make a first impression. In fact, in a Princeton study, psychologists Alexander Todorov and Janine Willis found that "our brains decide whether a person is attractive and trustworthy within a tenth of a second" by the "face's character." Your cover letter is the face of your business plan, so make sure it has the right character.

Your main focus should be on your audience and how you want to be perceived. Consider fonts, colors, and designs that will be true to you and appeal to them, and set the tone for the rest of the business plan to be consistent. I like to "KISS" (keep it simple, stupid). Your cover letter is important to make that impression, but simple.

Call To Action

My business' cover letter is its Start To Success Formula. This is the 5-step, proven process to understand who, what, where, why, and how to create your knowledge business... and take your life back today! If you think something's missing, when is NOW! Don't delay your future for another day.

iquitmyjobtohelpyouquityours.com/start-to-success-formula

Exercise

1. What is the name of your company?

2. What is your contact info such as website, physical address, e-mail, and phone?

3. What is your logo?

4. How much and from whom would you be raising money

5. What is your "elevator pitch?" (this should be 10-20 seconds describing what benefit your company provides to its customers)

Summary

"My favorite things in life don't cost any money. It's really clear that the most precious resource we all have is time."

Steve Jobs

My business was a very simple concept to start, and I think a lot of people would do great by starting their knowledge business consulting on some expertise that they already have. Working one-on-one gives a lot of insight into what people really want. After putting in my 10,000+ hours, which is how long Malcom Gladwell says it takes to achieve mastery in a field in his book *Outliers*, I had mastery in a field that many do not. I just had to package and market it in a way that added enough value to my customers to be profitable.

One of my business heroes, Marcus Lemonis, says that we should all do our best to avoid putting on a façade as entrepreneurs. He means that, when we go into business for ourselves, there is a temptation to appear "successful," but pretending to be someone you're not just adds stress and confusion. That's why I want to be 100% **genuine and vulnerable** in my life. Instead of pretending to not need help, I'll focus my energy seeking out people who can all help each other.

A recent Pew Research Center study found that roughly 30% of the U.S. workforce is made up by self-employed individuals and those that they hire (small businesses). [6] As technology makes it easier for individuals to share knowledge with a wide reach and laser focus at the same time, opportunity for consultants and other teachers will increase.

One step further is that knowledge workers don't need an organization at all. But you will always have relationships in your business. If you present your business plan to someone, your summary is the most important part. If your audience doesn't love your summary, they won't read beyond it. On the other hand, if your summary is organized and grabs their attention, you can direct the reader's focus to the points that you want to make.

The best way to grab someone's attention is to simply show them why your knowledge business will succeed. You can summarize a SWOT analysis—internal strengths and weaknesses, and external opportunities and threats—that we will cover in detail in the Market section. Once you have their attention, show the benefit to them—your business as a good investment. Show how they will get a return on their investment with a summary of the financial forecast that we will cover in detail in the Finances section.

It is good practice to write the summary after you've completed the rest of your business plan. Even though it comes first, it is easiest to write once you've completed your detailed material. You'll know what's important, and you can highlight it here. Have a good reason if you make it longer than a page or two. A good rule is to have one page of writing and one of financial highlights.

Exercise

1.   What is your biggest strength?

2.   What is your biggest weakness, and how are you going to hedge against it?

3.   What is the biggest opportunity for your business?

4.   What are specific threats to your industry or company, and how are you going to hedge?

5.   What differentiates you from your competitors?

6.   How long before your investors recoup their initial investment?

7.   What can your investors expect after that?

Company

*"The companies we admire are like the people
we admire: resilient, authentic, personable,
collaborative, ambitious, and humble."*

Chip Conley

If I were pitching my business right now, I couldn't talk about its illustrious past, millions of customers, and impact to the global economy. It doesn't have much of a history, so instead, I would turn the focus to myself. I ran a profitable franchise, an unprofitable e-commerce company, I have deep education and experience in business finances, and I've worked with many other businesses and individuals to help plan and create value. All of this gives me some good knowledge on what works and what doesn't.

An investor may still be skeptical, because the business itself doesn't have a long track record. But because I've already highlighted my personal track record, the attention shifts to me and my team. If I can show a proof of concept—that what I have to offer is valuable to people, even if a small number—then an investor may be interested in how we can grow that concept.

If we've shifted the focus to my team, then there's a gap in that it's a small one—in fact, full-time, it's just me! I bridge this gap by having my mentor, Bill, as an advisor, who has an impressive track record. Also, my business model draws on the expertise of my customers regarding their wheelhouse, which dictates their customer and product. Especially anyone I work with one-on-one are all my partners, and therefore, part of my team. This is all valuable to my company.

According to the March, 2016 U.S. Bureau of Labor Statistics report, 15 million people (10.1% of U.S. workers) were self-employed in 2015 (these are the business owners). Interestingly, the overall self-employment trend has decreased from 12.1% in 1994. However, the report states that this reflects the massive shift in the agricultural sector from family farms to large corporations and replacing human labor with machines.[7]

The opportunity I see with this business reflects the overall advancement in technology: It is now easier and cheaper to launch a business than ever before, and it can be done quickly and responsively using a feedback loop. I intend my business to play a role in this movement to Drucker's **knowledge society** by providing education, entertainment, and partnerships along the way.

In this section, paint a picture of your business' past, present, and future. Right now, you won't have a past, so focus on you and any team you want to build. Discuss past education and experience that positions you for success, just as I did above. Include your investor in the future of the company and discuss how you see the relationship continuing. Showing that the two of you are on the same team right away is a great way to start the relationship.

Highlight the opportunity that the company faces and how it translates into longer term goals (1, 5, and 10-years is a good place to start). How did you get to where you are today, and how do these goals translate into what you want the company to become? You want your audience to see the potential that you see for your company. Once you've shown the company from a high level and evoked some emotion, you can give the details found in this chapter's exercise.

Exercise

1. What is your mission statement?

2. What is your company's legal form (LLC etc.)?

3. What is your state/jurisdiction of formation?

4. What is your tax identification number?

5. What is the company's fiscal year?

6. For bookkeeping, do you have a CPA? What system or service do you use?

7. What insurance do you have that mitigate industry-specific risks?

Product/Service

"The only way to advertise is by not focusing on the product."

Calvin Klein

The concept for my products are simple: I help employees take charge of their lives by providing a roadmap to create a knowledge business. For many people, the benefit of this is priceless (I know it is for me). To be in charge of your own business, career, and day-to-day life is no small thing. Our current education system teaches us how to be good employees, so being a business owner is elusive to many. I help people understand the benefits of owning their own business, transition their mindset, and building something of value.

Executing on this concept is a little more complex, as it always is. Obviously, one of my products is this book, and I use this as a way to start a relationship with customers. I foresee future books as well that will cover different areas but have the same overall goal. Then, I use the various product forms discussed in the Back Of The Napkin chapter to maximize the value I provide to my customers.

In the first paragraph of this chapter, notice that I didn't say how I help my customers do market research or forecast financial statements. I didn't talk about how anyone can form an LLC or that registering with state and local tax agencies isn't that tough. I definitely didn't talk about best-practice management and bookkeeping processes. And I didn't mention the importance of marketing funnels or digital presence.

I led with the outcome, or **benefit**, that I provide to my customers. A previous Harvard Business School professor, Theodore Levitt, summarized this concept with the famous quote "People don't want to buy a quarter-inch drill. They want a quarter-inch hole!" People buy a better future from you. What kind of future do you want to provide?

To differentiate your business plan, and make it a persuasive one, lead this section with the benefit that your product provides to your target customer. What is the reward that they get or pain they avoid by using your product? This should clearly reflect the market research that you've done. One of the easiest ways to come up with your product is to see what your market is already buying from **competitors**, and then ask your market what it's missing.

If you can convince someone to become a customer of yours, then it's just one step further to get an investor. If you were pitching to an investor, you would give an overview of how you make your product and get it into customer hands. You will go into more detail in the strategy and finance sections about necessary equipment, personnel needed, and cost.

If you have multiple products (plan on it), give an overview of them, but focus on the one that your forecast predicts will have the most impact in the near future. If you have tons of potential products, categorize them and talk about product lines. Discuss any relationships between your products, especially if some are complements or substitutes.

Finally, go over key features of the product. Approach this discussion with the objective of showing how your product differs from competitors'. If there are any distinct differences, this can prompt the conversation of intellectual property. Discuss any IP that you own or have pending and how you see it affecting your risk. If you don't intend to obtain any, discuss why.

Call To Action

My passion is to help people like you make the leap from employee to entrepreneur by building a knowledge business from scratch, so I will continue to work one-on-one with a small number of people.

I'm especially excited about some content that I can only allude to here. Basically, I want to share even more stories about people making this leap.

If you have an idea and are serious about starting your own business, but you want a partner who's done it before, I can work with you. My next client could be you!

Visit iquitmyjobtohelpyouquityours.com/inner-circle

Exercise

1. What benefit does your product provide?

2. How does your product differ from competitors'?

3. What are key features of your product?

4. What, if anything, should you consider protecting with intellectual property?

5. What are your product lines or categories?

6. If you have multiple product lines, what percentage of sales do you expect each to drive?

Market

"The more people I help, the more successful I am."

Robert Kiyosaki

Mr. Kiyosaki is most widely known as the author of *Rich Dad Poor Dad*, and this attitude is one of the reasons I look up to him. I try to follow this message, and that's why I always want to make content available for free. It's also why I want to leverage technology to make my services available to more than the people that I work with one-on-one—many more I hope. However, I didn't plan to conquer the world in one day, so I started with a niche.

I picked my niche by looking at what I was good at, enjoyed, and what market I understood. I think I know myself better than anyone else, so I started there. I knew how I felt working at large companies, not challenged, appreciated, or a master of my own destiny. I wanted to take control and create a positive impact. This was the story I had to tell, and, if I stuck to my story, it would be easy to be authentic every step of the way.

As Einstein said, "a man should look for what is, and not for what he thinks should be." It didn't take much thought or research to confirm that there were others who felt the same as me. Instead of wishing and wanting, I recognized what "is." Then I felt confident in delivering a message with the goal of changing things into what I thought "should be." Remember how this book started with a definition of "entrepreneur?" This is how I could shape the world—or at least a small piece of it—in my own image.

There are plenty of businesses out there that will create a business plan, and there are even online services that keep data available for you to update your plan. The way I saw to differentiate myself was 1) whom I was targeting, and 2) that these people were doing the "what" work, and I wanted to do the "how" and "why." It's easy to go online and find a business plan template, but understanding why it's important and how to create it in a way that will help drive your vision is a different story, and that's what I want to tell.

I didn't necessarily think that I would be getting into the "business coaching" industry, but this is probably the best description of what I do. That industry continues to trend up for mainly two reasons:

1) Entrepreneurs are often looking for organization, focus, and to reveal dangerous gaps in their knowledge, and
2) Employees are looking for productivity, leadership skills, and key moves to climb in their careers.

I place myself as a bridge across the divide, helping those employees who realize the climb is no longer what they desire, and who need to gain a new skillset quickly.

Moving into your market analysis, organize into three main areas—customers, industry, and competitors. The SWOT analysis, that we mentioned in the Summary, is very useful here. To differentiate your business plan and make it something great, don't just jump into percentages and other statistics. While this is important, it's better to lead with a description of your target market that makes it clear that you know these people through and through.

Customers

Talk about your ideal customers' deepest fears and desires. "Ideal" means the person that your business is best suited to help, the ones in your wheelhouse. Operate under the assumption that you can't reach everyone, so make the hard decisions around whom you really want to go after. Remember that you're not selling your customers a product; you're selling them an outcome, future, or state of being.

Create a customer avatar that describes these people from their income to their education, work, family, hobbies, location, habits, and anything else relevant to show how and why they want your product. Remember what Mr. Drucker said: The purpose of a business is to create a customer, so the first step to success is showing that people will demand your product.

I recommend you start with a **niche**, but, if and when there are deviations from your ideal customer, explain the different demographics, and show what percentage of your business will be made up by these different segments. Are you targeting multiple segments with different products or services? Show which segments will make up what percentage of sales by product. Are there trends in these customers' spending habits?

Industry

Now that you understand your customer, look at your industry from a high level by discussing overall trends. Because you're competing online, this should cover your entire country (or anyone who speaks your language) and other businesses that don't provide the exact same product as you, but maybe they provide substitute products. Be humble; don't think that your customers couldn't live without you! If they couldn't get your product, where would they go?

The online education market is around $100 billion annually and going up right now. Research the market for the past few years and expert projections in the upcoming years. Research your wheelhouse trends. An upward trend is generally thought to be a good thing, but this usually creates additional competition as well. A downward trend isn't necessarily bad news. If other companies are exiting the market because of difficulties, this could be a great place to capitalize, especially if you're putting a unique twist on your product.

Once you've set the stage for the industry as a whole, go into your relevant market, which is the set of customers that you actually intend to go after and how much they would spend with you. If you were previously showing your industry across all English speakers, now focus on those most likely to understand and demand your product.

Approach your market size from two main angles:

1) **Customer-centric** – show your relevant market size in number of potential customers, and
2) **Product-centric** – show it in units of product sold. Calculate total annual revenue that your market would generate for your business. You can foreshadow your finances section by giving worst, likely, and best case scenarios for market share, because this will drive your revenue.

Competitors

Now that you've laid out your industry, go into how your competitors fit into it. If your product is cutting edge, stretch your research, and your imagination, to consider how other companies could compete for your business. It is better to look at companies that, on the surface, don't appear to be direct competitors, but do your research, rather than miss a valid consideration. The key here is to understand your competitors and clearly show what **differentiates** your business.

Then move into statistics around these competitors. Show whom the big players in your market are and the percentages of market share that they control? Identify if certain companies skew to one segment or another, and highlight any opportunities that you intend to take advantage of. Illustrate any trends in the competitive landscape, and highlight any threats or opportunities that you see in a growing or dying competitor.

Call To Action

Want to start researching your competition right now? Even if we're not direct competitors, you can see exactly what I'm doing by heading to my website!

Visit iquitmyjobtohelpyouquityours.com

Exercise

1. Look back to the Summary chapter. Has your SWOT analysis changed?

2. Who is your ideal customer? Create a customer avatar. Name your customer and create his bio.

3. What were overall industry sales in the past few years?

4. What do experts expect them to be in upcoming years?

5. What is driving this trend?

6. What is the population count of your relevant market?

7. What number of units are sold to your relevant market each year?

8. What total sales does your relevant market drive each year?

9. What percentage of this market do you expect to grab?

Exercise Continued

10. Fill out a pie chart below that shows your competitors' % of your relevant market.

Competitor % of Relevant Market

Strategy

"A satisfied customer is the best business strategy of all."

Michael LeBoeuf

As I shared in the Overview section, I shape my business strategy around the life I want to lead: I want to be free to work from anywhere, have a variety of projects that keep me learning, and make serious, positive impact on as many people as possible. Per Mr. LeBoeuf, if I can keep satisfied customers this way, then I'm in business.

We've already talked some about my products, but let's look at correctly pricing and delivering them. Starting with my one-on-one consulting, I looked at my competitors. Depending on the scope of the engagement, I learned that it made sense to charge $2,000 - $10,000 per month. One big point for me was that I didn't want to charge an hourly rate; I wanted my client to know the cost, and then I would over-deliver on value. This also makes for a more predictable business.

When I decided that I wanted to scale my service in a boot camp style and other forms (including this book), I had to reconsider pricing. Again, I went to my competitors, but I also recognized that I was delivering similar content to my consulting, just with less personal interaction. The guiding light I try to follow is to deliver **ten times the value** of what I charge for it (the 10X rule). Obviously, this is subjective, but if you're honest with yourself, I don't think you can go wrong this way.

With social media these days, it's relatively easy to get your knowledge products in front of enough people to test the demand of them. It's also easy to split-test ideas to refine pricing and other components. Fortunately, I've been in this market as a consumer longer than a provider (I've taken most of the good courses out there), so I knew whom I wanted to target and how to phrase my message. In general, I want to find abundant-minded people who decide for change, and are willing to learn, implement, and adapt. I look to social media giants like Tai Lopez for help with this (I got the 10X rule from him).

In a 2012 Forbes article titled "Strategy 101: It's All About Alignment," author Larry Miler states that "65% of organizations have an agreed-upon strategy. 14% of employees understand the organization's strategy. Less than 10% of all organizations successfully execute the strategy." This shows that a lot of difficulties arise from people in the company not being on the same page. This may not be as relevant while your company is small, but the main takeaway for me was to ensure that your strategy aligns 1) what your customers want, 2) what you're selling, and 3) the message that's selling it.

The strategy section is your opportunity to look to the future. A lot of your time may be spent executing, but this is the time to strategize. If you create a good strategy and consider variables, then you will be able to focus on what's important and execute in your daily routine. Remember that a strategy is not carved in stone, and you should revisit it regularly and when presented with new information. Divide your strategy into two sections—marketing and operations.

Marketing Strategy

Remember that marketing is not just advertising; it refers to any action for promotion and sales. As you work through your marketing strategy, keep your **brand** in mind. What kind of company do you want to be? What do you want to be known for? What do you want people to think of when they see you? For structure, I recommend that you focus your marketing strategy on the four Ps: These are product, pricing, promotion, and placement.

Product/Service

You already covered the details of your product's benefits and features. Now you need to discuss how your business plans to manage changes, releases, and innovation. Discuss where your business will focus at the beginning and how this will change as it hits various milestones in the future, and talk about complementary products that you have or plan to release into the future. Highlight industry trends and how they are affecting the evolution of products. Talk about the necessity for continuing education and research and development.

Pricing

Correctly pricing your product can be one of the most difficult things to do, unless you have a comparable competitor to base it on. Even then, you should consider how you will differentiate, and price will play a role in this. When determining the right price for a product, focus on two main things—**value and experimentation**.

In the same way that you're thinking about your product as the benefit it provides instead of the features it has, think of the value that it adds to your customer's life instead of just a price tag. New entrepreneurs tend to price things too low. I know you want to be fair; just remember that lower prices suggest lower value, whether it's true or not. Do your research, and recognize your value. You are worth it!

One of the best things you can do is experiment with your prices. The best way to do this is with split testing, which is easy to do online. Raising or lowering your price may not always have the impact on overall sales that you expect. The rule in marketing is to always test. Ultimately, you want to find the pricing that adds the most perceived value to your customers and the most profit to your business.

Promotion

Your discussion around promotion should tie directly back to your market. Talk about your ideal customers using your avatar, and show that you know exactly how to reach them. Additionally, show that you know how your competitors promote and how that may impact your efforts. By taking both sides of the market into account, you should be able to discuss the exact media you intend to use.

Aside from customers and competitors, discuss any industry-specific considerations, such as seasonality in your market that suggests spending more on advertising at a certain time of year. If you're leveraging word-of-mouth (including online shares, likes etc.), highlight the reasons that people are incentivized to talk about you. Looking at trends in your market, politics, legislation, and the environment, show how your approach to your customers is appropriate.

What is your message going to be? Again, think of your brand and how you want to be perceived by potential customers. Look again at the title of this book. It's clear what my message is, right? It's okay to turn some people off with your marketing, in fact, it's a great strategy. Be true to yourself, and be edgy enough that some people say "no thanks," but people that resonate with you can't wait to learn more.

Placement

Start this section by again focusing on your ideal customers. Where do they look for your product? Show your product where people are **already looking for it**. Discuss exactly how you're going to get your product into your customers' hands. Will you ship them a book? Will people log into a website? Will you use YouTube? Will they download everything? Do your customers need to schedule a time to speak with you in person?

Also, show your product where people are, but be very careful to target people who would be interested in your product. This is why TV advertising is dying for a lot of businesses, and yet it's a great idea for a company selling a revolutionary denture product to put ads in daytime TV. Facebook and other digital marketing opportunities allow you to target an audience that is already interested in what you have to offer, and then they see it throughout the normal course of their day.

In a successful business, acquiring a customer is just the beginning. The real value comes when you keep customers for life. You want your brand name to be first in their mind when they need your product. Show your investors how you are going to justify the cost of acquiring a customer by creating much more value for your business than just one sale. How will guide them up the Customer Impact graph?

Exercise

1. What are the trends in your market, and how have products evolved?

2. Fill out a pie chart below that shows what percentage of revenue will come from your top three products.

Product Mix

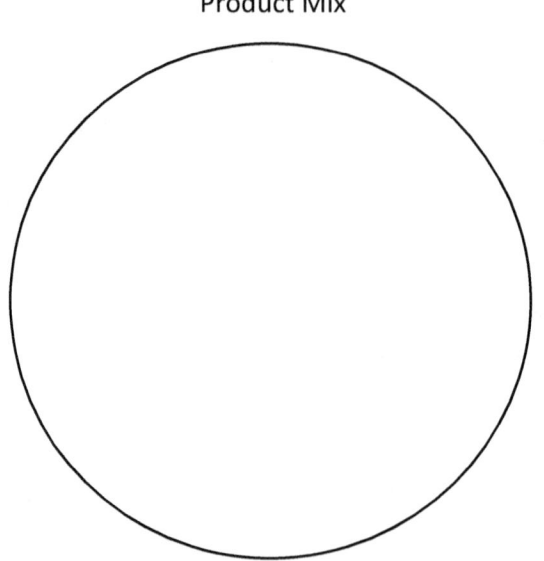

3. How will you price each of your initial products?

Exercise Continued

4. Fill out a pie chart below that shows where you will acquire your customers from (word of mouth, paid advertising, organic traffic...)

Customer Acquisition

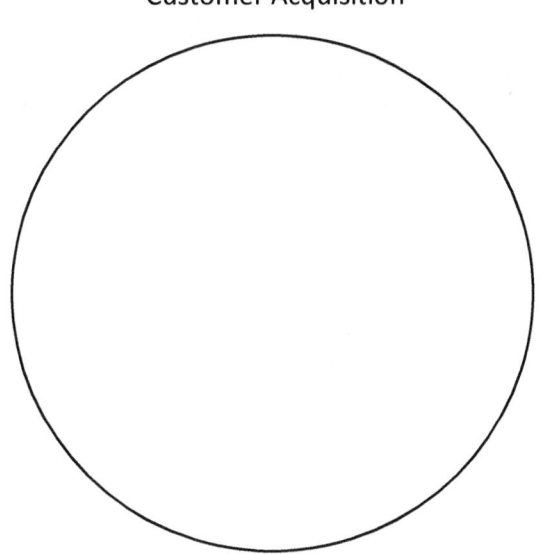

5. Describe the process of getting a purchase into a customer's hands.

Operations Strategy

"Operations" sounds so broad that it's almost abstract. Your operations strategy should cover how your business will create something out of nothing, in a sense. Without your business, there wouldn't be your team's effort, capital investment in equipment and education, and a new entity in existence. Now that your business exists, how are you going to create a product that someone wants, and how are you going to do it efficiently and profitably? For structure, I recommend that you focus your operations strategy on two sections—daily operations and milestones.

Daily Operations

This is the time to be specific about the actual function of your business. Discuss the different departments in your business and their respective responsibilities. Focus on their primary function and how this contributes to the success of the whole. It's ok if this all starts out as a one-person-show, but look to the future of building a team. How you will attract and retain these people? Though there are many possible departments, I suggest you start with the four main expense lines on your profit and loss statement:

1) Cost of Goods Sold – people actually creating your product or providing your service
2) Sales & Marketing – people driving sales and promotion in some capacity
3) Research & development – people innovating new products
4) General & Administrative – support people in information technology, legal, human resources, and finance

Keeping these four areas in mind, you can decide which departments are relevant to your business. Most businesses should have finance, legal, HR, marketing, IT, operations, and admin departments, though some of these may be external from the business. For example, it's common that small businesses hire an external legal firm and accountant before they are big enough to have the demand for one inside the company. We'll discuss the core responsibilities to consider in the upcoming Team section.

Once you've laid out the structure of your business, discuss the key processes that must take place on a regular basis. This includes your sales process which details how your business generates leads and turns them into satisfied customers that keep coming back. It includes your delivery process that details the logistics of distributing your product or service. I could write an entire book on all the potential inner operations of a business, and maybe I will... but you should consider what needs to happen for your business to work on an ongoing basis, and detail this out.

Milestones

This is the time to look to the future and identify key markers along your business' path. Think about what you want to accomplish with your business and what will demonstrate success along the way, to both you and your investors. Break out how you will achieve these milestones with **SMART** goals along the way (defined in the following paragraph). And be sure to highlight the key **assumptions** that you're making.

What are SMART goals? Let's use the always popular example: A dumb goal would be "I want to lose weight." A smart one would be "I want to lose 10 pounds of fat in 3 months after the holidays." When you create goals, ensure that you can define each piece of it.

- Specific – 10 pounds of fat
- Measurable – I can use a scale to know if I'm successful or not (and track along the way)
- Achievable – Depending on details, most experts would agree 1 pound /week is very possible
- Realistic – I'm considering my situation, and I know I can't do this during the holidays
- Time-bound – 3 months

Some example milestones would be book or other product releases, breaking even financially (where your income covers your expenses), making key connections, media attention, levels of profit, fundraising, and investor return. The milestones your business will reach is limited only by your imagination, so focus on the steps that will be in-line with your promise to yourself and other stakeholders in the business. Also, make sure they are consistent with your daily operations.

Exercise

1. Add dates and milestones to the timeline below (ex. "book release" or "$10K /month revenue.")

Strategic Roadmap

_____

2. What SMART goals will help you achieve each of these milestones? (Make your goals specific, measurable, achievable, realistic, and time-bound.)

3. What key assumptions are you making for each milestone that would significantly alter your strategic roadmap if different?

Call To Action

Want to know what my #1 goal and strategy is? Everything I do points towards my membership site, where we're building a community of like-minded individuals who want to better themselves and others.

Curious what that looks like? We hope you're our next member!

Visit iquitmyjobtohelpyouquityours.com/members

Team

When I was leaving my last job, one of my colleagues asked what I would miss the most. Especially coming from this lovely young woman whom I respect and admire, the answer to that question was very simple: I would miss the people. When I think about the amount of time that I spent with some of my past colleagues, it amazes me to realize that it's more than I spend with my parents, my niece, or even my fiancé on a day-to-day basis.

Working a 9-5, which, in my experience, is actually more like an 8-6, or sometimes a 7-7 or more, I spent an incredible amount of time around my colleagues. Additionally, my personality makes me very comfortable in social settings, so I knew it would be a big transition working on my own for a while. That's why I planned two things while still at my job:

1) I developed relationships with more established consulting firms that I could do some work with. This would allow me to learn from them but also interact with them and their clients.
2) I planned from the beginning that this would only be a one man show for so long. As I'm writing this book, I've already started hiring people, though mostly just for support or one-time projects that are outside my expertise.

This second point brings up the concept of **outsourcing**, and for someone like me, it's an amazing thing to be able to fill an immediate labor demand by going online and making a connection. Some of these one-time deals lead to longer-term relationships, so I have more and more people that I can rely on for quality work. As my products continues to evolve, and my crusade continues, I look forward to building a tribe that is as excited about my message as I am.

In its global outsourcing survey 2016, Deloitte stated that "disruption in the form of cloud-based services is just the start: we are on the verge of an entirely new model of service delivery comprising robotic and cognitive process automation, the 'internet of things,' and digital IT management. This intersection of traditional outsourcing and the innovation storm could amplify value for those organizations that can correctly harness it, and this will likely lead to ever increasing uses of outsourcing, even as it reinvents itself."[9]

No matter the size or source, you and, when the time comes, your team are what will make your business successful, and it is what others will invest in. This section is your opportunity to demonstrate your team's expertise and ability. Start with yourself, but then look to the future. Who are the people that are going to make decisions that will significantly impact the direction of the business? Discuss their education, qualifications, and experience as it is relevant.

You may worry about not having a track record. You can overcome this obstacle by finding someone who has done it before to be a mentor and advisor for your business. This doesn't have to be terribly formal, but just having someone to bounce questions off will be immensely helpful, and it will instill confidence in others. Then the discussion moves to "Yes this is our first business, but here is why we're qualified to run it, and we have expert guidance."

My mentor, Bill, is doing this for me: I meet with him on a quarterly basis for a business lunch, and he's always available for a quick e-mail or call as well. Remember that advice is like… a heart: Everyone has one. So, while it can be useful to bounce ideas off anyone that you trust and respect, seek out someone who has done what you're trying to do, and their advice will be invaluable.

Exercise

1. Enter your team's names in the boxes below. This concept, from *The E-Myth Revisited*, ensures that the core team has clear roles. If your name is in all the boxes starting out, that's ok, but it's important to set expectations, and it may change over time. The team should fill this out together and work out obvious imbalances. Add on any additional, necessary roles as well.[10]

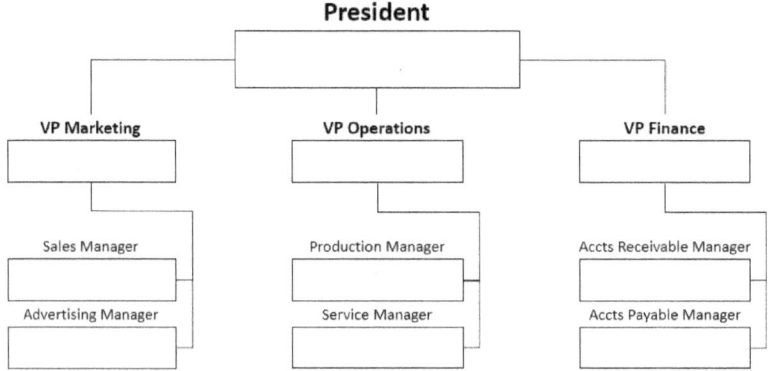

2. What is your one-paragraph bio? Plan to get everyone on your management team, advisory board, and all owners to create one of these.

Call To Action

Is the concept of a team appealing to you? Do you want to make something happen for yourself, but you need that social support? Well you can get that and hands-on attention for your business.

Our boot camps are the closest thing to one-on-one at a lower cost and with the benefit of building comradery with the people you build your business with to boot...

Visit iquitmyjobtohelpyouquityours.com/boot-camp

Finances

Because I spent my corporate career in finance and accounting, this area was high on my list of things to consider, but I'm probably an exception. A lot of entrepreneurs get into a business because they have a passion for the work, and that's definitely something we need more of in this world. This goes back to inspiration, which is essential to success, but so is a very practical view of your business finances.

At the risk of sounding like a hypocrite, I quit my job before I had enough income from my business to cover my expenses. However, I had saved enough money to last 12 months with anticipated expenses. I considered this to be pretty conservative, and maybe you will go about it slightly differently. But I do recommend you build your business on the side at first, and I'll also say that unexpected expenses seem to always creep up.

I kept my expenses down by having a home office and visiting client sites when necessary. I did my best to distinguish between an "expense" and an "investment." Though these aren't technical definitions, I think of an **expense** as something that's just necessary to keep the machine running whereas I think of an **investment** as something that will improve my business and my life. I want to keep expenses as low as possible, but I will spend any amount of money if I'm convinced it will increase my knowledge or help my business in the long-term.

Some coaches and consultants work on a project, track their hours, and then bill their client at the end of the week or month. I took a course from a great consultant, Sam Ovens, who got me in the mindset to package any service I provided into a dollar amount that would be paid up-front or on an on-going basis, just like a product. As discussed earlier, this would ensure that both parties knew the dollar amount involved and my focus was on providing value greater than that amount.

Finance and accounting are very complex. There's a reason that "The Big 4" accounting firms earned a combined $124 billion and employed nearly 1 million employees in 2015. And these are just the largest of these firms that provide audit and other services to the tens of thousands of companies around the world, all of which have their own finance departments.

Accounting has all kinds of rules that are meant to recognize revenues when they are "earned," and to recognize expenses in the period that "matches" the related revenue. However, for you, there is one area that is paramount: Remember that **cash is king**. More technically, this area is called cash flow. Cash flow is just what it sounds like: It's the money flowing in and out of your business. To demonstrate its importance for even a profitable business, let's use an example.

If my business sold custom motorcycles, and today we made a $20K sale, drinks are on me, right? Except what if we don't get paid until we deliver the bike? First I have to purchase all the right parts, pay my expert team to manufacture it, and afford all the normal overhead like rent and utilities in the meantime. Let's assume, after all is said and done, we make $5K per bike.

If this was the company's first sale, we better have started with enough money to cover all those expenses prior to collecting from our customer (in this case $15K). Now imagine that word gets out how amazing our bikes are, and we get another $100K in sales for 5 bikes. This growth is amazing, right? But now we have $20K in the bank and need to cover $75K in expenses.

In the same US Bank study that was referenced in the What This Book is About section, the #1 financial—and overall—factor for small business failure was "poor cash flow management skills". The example above is how businesses—even those with high demand and growth potential—get into cash flow problems.

One of the beautiful things about your knowledge business is that it involves minimal investment up front, and you don't have many expenses to deliver to your customers. When you're planning the finances of your business, focus on how you will have enough cash in the bank to cover your expenses as you profit and grow. There are many ways to do this, but here are a few of the major ones to consider whenever possible:

1) Collect from your customers quickly, or even get cash up-front
2) Pay your vendors slowly, or once you actually benefit from your purchase
3) Don't over-invest in inventory for bulk discounts – ensure it will sell first
4) Only invest in new equipment when it will increase quality and profitability
5) Purchase software as a service to have small, monthly fees, instead of large, up-front costs

Remember that finance can also be a verb, and if you get to the stage where you want someone to finance growth in your venture, I recommend you organize your finances into two sections—use of funds and financial analysis. When you're starting out, focus more on the first section and how you will use your start-up money (whatever its source) to arrive at a break-even point.

Use of Funds

Start this section by recapping how much money you intend to start the business with. Then go over how that money will be used. Distinguish between start-up capital and working capital:

1) Start-up capital includes everything you need to open shop. For your knowledge business, this could include licenses, computer, phone, video recording equipment, website, and marketing software.
2) Working capital includes everything you need to keep the business going in the short-term, including software expenses and your salary (yes you will need to continue paying rent and other bills!)

Start-up capital will be used up before there's any chance of a return, so this is another great time to stress the advantage of a knowledge business. However, the amount needed can still differ, so be sure you take the time to determine what you will need to invest up-front.

Working capital will be required on an on-going basis. Its technical definition is current assets minus current liabilities, which basically demonstrates how much liquidity you have. Ensure that your plan allows more money to be coming in than is going out. This may sound simple, but as demonstrated in the example above, it takes good planning, not just a good product.

Financial Analysis

Here, you should highlight top-line revenue, key expenses, and income for the next 3-5 years. Remember that an investor wants to know that he will see a return, so draw attention to 1) your break-even point, and 2) the point at which any investors will see their return on investment. You can save detailed documents such as balance sheet, income statement, and statement of cash flows for the appendix.

Your **break-even point** is extremely important, because this signifies a sustainable business. If your sales equal your expenses—and your expenses include your salary—then the business will survive forever. This is comforting for owners and investors alike, because it means that any additional profit is a return of one kind or another.

Return on investment can come in many different forms, but I recommend that you aim to get returns in the following order:

1) Pay pre-existing commitments to investors or others
2) Re-invest in growth for the business' long-term
3) Pay out appropriate bonuses for all your hard work

The order of these is important! When things start going well, we all have the instinct to celebrate, and we assume the good times will last forever. But we also need to prepare for that roller coaster to head down. I believe that the moment you stop investing in your business and considering how it must change and adapt for the future, your business stops working for you. Then it isn't long before it stops working altogether.

Call To Action

With my CPA and background in finance, you can bet I'll use that strength to help you get a grasp in this area of business and life. Filling in those general business gaps all starts with the Start To Success Formula, though. First, you have to know where the gaps are!

iquitmyjobtohelpyouquityours.com/start-to-success-formula

Exercise

1. How much start-up capital do you need?

2. How much working capital will you need on a monthly basis?

3. How will you collect payment from your customers, and how long will it take?

4. Fill out the following financial forecast highlight. This is a simplified version of a profit and loss, or income statement, which will be in your appendix. The most important thing here is to critically consider the relationship between A, B, and E. Understanding your gross margin and operating expenses is essential to profitability.

Exercise Continued

	Year 1	Year 2	Year 3
Sales (A)	$	$	$
Cost of Sales (B)	$	$	$
Gross Margin (C = A-B)	$	$	$
Gross Margin % (D = C/A)		%	%	%
Operating Expenses			
Payroll	$	$	$
Rent	$	$	$
Utilities	$	$	$
Insurance	$	$	$
Supplies	$	$	$
Other	$	$	$
Total Operating Expenses (E)	$	$	$
Net Profit (F = C-E)	$	$	$

5. What is your break-even point in year 1? This is the amount of sales that you need to reach to cover your expenses and have a $0 net profit. Calculate this as E/D. Again, this is a simplified calculation (excluding items like tax and interest), but it is extremely effective to keep a finger on your financial pulse.

Exit Strategy

"Twenty years from now, you will be more disappointed by the things that you didn't do than by the ones you did do. So throw off the bowlines. Sail away from the safe harbor. Catch the trade winds in your sails. Explore. Dream. Discover."

Mark Twain

Twenty years from now, I still want to be helping people build successful businesses based around their strengths and passions. I have no doubt that my business will look different then, but I intend to continue working with people to this end until the day I die. Retirement has no appeal to me. Playing more golf? Sure. Working fewer hours? Probably. But why would I ever stop doing what I'm good at, what I enjoy, and what I think is my best way to make the world a better place?

I'm definitely considering how certain areas of my work could be segmented into different businesses down the line, and I want to be able to hand over the reins whenever I'm no longer the best suited to run one of them. For example, once certain digital programs that I've created are "finalized," it may make sense to step away and have someone else manage them.

I will also earn "sweat equity" in some of the companies that I help people start. When appropriate, part of my fee will be in some kind of equity or other long-term benefit instead of cash. This will be with the intent of investing in those that I help and growing and profiting with them. But there will come a time when it will make the most sense for these entrepreneurs to take full ownership back.

There are many possible ways to exit a business. This is a section that many people skip, and some are even insulted or afraid to include it. However, you don't have to be a Silicon Valley start-up master with a 3-year plan to give proof of concept, raise capital, build a minimally viable product, and get acquired by Google or Facebook for this to be an important part of this planning exercise. Your exit strategy could be to run a profitable practice until a ripe old age and then have someone else run the day-to-day and retain ownership even when you "retire."

Whatever your exit strategy, it is extremely valuable to include this section. It makes you consider the long-term, and it shows others that you expect that long-term to be profitable for you and anyone else on your team. This exercise can also be a great way to bring you full circle, back to our chapter on finding your inspiration. It will make you reflect on why you want to start this business and what you hope to achieve with it.

Exercise

1. What do you want to accomplish before exiting your business?

2. How old will you be?

3. How will you exit?

4. How many employees will you have?

5. What will your annual revenues be?

6. What will you be contributing to the world?

7. What will you do with your additional time?

Call To Action

All things are temporary. So, know that the hard times will pass, and enjoy the things you love. Our community would love to hear about how you intend to exit your job, though...

Visit facebook.com/groups/starttosuccess

Appendices

In an attempt to come full circle, let's remind ourselves of something we covered in the Cover Letter: KISS stands for "keep it simple, stupid." I'm not arrogant enough to say that your business is simple, or that starting any business is simple for that matter. However, when planning, do your best to keep your eye on what's really important—providing the best product, value, and experience to your customer at a profit.

One way to keep the actual document for your business plan simple and straight to the point is to have a section for appendices at the end. Below are common appendices that you should have available at any presentation of your business plan. What you have in the main sections of your plan versus an appendix can vary based on your business and your audience, so instead of using the list below as a hard-and-fast rule, just ask yourself this question: "For my goal with this plan today, where is this information most effective, and how should I present it?"

You can reference these items throughout your business plan. You can jump to them when asked, cover them at the end of your presentation, or not use them at all. If something isn't relevant to achieve your goal, then ignore it, but still include it in an appendix. This level of preparation will add to your confidence and competence, and others will see this.

Company

- Formation papers
- Business license
- Operating agreement
- Important insurance agreements
- Picture(s) of place of operations

Product/Service

- Your product, prototype or offer
- Supply chain flow chart
- Intellectual property documentation such as patents

Market

- Expert market trend predictions
- Competitor summaries
- Ideal customer avatar

Strategy

- Strategic roadmap
- Product pricing list

Team

- Other biographies
- Attorney summary
- Accountant summary

Finances

- Cash flow statements
- Income statements
- Balance sheets

Conclusion

"The more people have studied different methods of bringing up children the more they have come to the conclusion that what good mothers and fathers instinctively feel like doing for their babies is the best after all."

Benjamin Spock

In a lot of ways, your business is like a child: First, you're just planning it with your partner, then you launch and all hell breaks loose. After that, there are some hard days and sleepless nights while you work diligently away, but it all seems worth it as you see it grow. If you're able to change and adapt as your relationship develops, it will start to run itself. Then, one day, it may take care of you.

The purpose of this book is to help you plan your knowledge business. But that is just one step in the journey of business ownership. If there are just **10 key points** that I can have you take away from this book, here they are:

1) Create a business for **your reasons**
2) Create it around your **strengths**
3) Create it around something that you're **passionate** and **curious** about
4) Get **help** from someone who has done what you're trying to do
5) Know your **customers** better than they know themselves
6) Create a minimally viable product or proof of concept to **test** as quickly as possible
7) Listen to **feedback**, especially from your customers

8) Know your **break-even** point, and plan to get there ASAP
9) Accept what is and put your energy into the things you can **control**
10) Start with the end in mind and think about the **life** you want to lead

As I conclude this book, I think of the people I hope to reach with it. I picture you in my head, and I wonder what you will accomplish with your business and with your life. There are too many possibilities to fathom, and I'm excited to see how the world changes as more and more people remove their golden handcuffs and get to their lives' work. I am on a crusade to help drive that change. Let me know how I can help you do this.

Notes

Introduction

1. Peter F. Drucker. *The Essential Drucker*. Chapter 23: *A Century of Social Transformation—Emergence of Knowledge Society.* New York: HarperCollinsPublishers, 2001. Print.
2. Harris Poll. *Half of U.S. Working Adults Own or Want to Own Their Own Businesses, Finds University of Phoenix Survey.* 2014. Online.

What This Book Is About

3. Jessie Hagen. *How to Avoid the Most Common Reasons for Small Business Failure.* 2013. Online.

Inspiration

4. Intuit, Inc. *How to Avoid the Most Common Reasons for Small Business Failure.* 2010. Online.

Cover Letter

5. Eric Wargo. *How Many Seconds to a First Impression?* 2006. Online.

Summary

6. PewResearchCenter. *Three-in-Ten U.S. Jobs Are Held by the Self-Employed and the Workers They Hire.* 2015. Online.

Company

7. Steven F. Hipple and Laurel A. Hammond. *Self-employment In The United States.* 2016. Online.

Strategy

8. Larry Myler. *Strategy 101: It's All About Alignment.* 2012. Online.

Team

9. Deloitte & Touche LLP. *Global outsourcing survey 2016: Step on it! Outsourcing makes a beeline toward innovation.* 2016. Online.
10. Michael E. Gerber. *The E-Myth Revisited.* Chapter 14: *Your Organizational Strategy.* New York: HarperCollinsPublishers, 1995. Print.

www.ingramcontent.com/pod-product-compliance
Lightning Source LLC
Chambersburg PA
CBHW070133210526
45170CB00013B/880